# real U

## GUIDE TO

# BUYING YOUR FIRST CAR

## JOHANNA BODNYK

# Real U Guides

**Publisher and CEO:**
Steve Schultz

**Editor-in-Chief:**
Megan Stine

**Art Director:**
C.C. Krohne

**Designer:**
David Jackson

**Illustration:**
Mike Strong

**Production Manager:**
Alice Todd

**Associate Editor:**
Cody O. Stine

**Editorial Assistant:**
Charles Bethea

Library of Congress Control Number: 2004090907

ISBN: 0-9744159-5-2

First Edition
10 9 8 7 6 5 4 3 2 1

Published by
Real U, Inc.
2582 Centerville Rosebud Rd.
Loganville, GA 30052

**www.realuguides.com**

Real U is a trademark of Real U, Inc.

**Photo Credits:**
Cover and Page 1: Photodisc Collection/Getty Images;
Page 3: Digital Vision/Getty Images; Page 4: Tony
Anderson/Getty Images; Page 5: Man and teen looking at car,
Marc Romanelli/Getty Images; Mini Cooper, Megan Stine;
Girl with keys, SW Productions/Getty Images; Page 6: Bruce
Ayres/Getty Images; Page 7: Lonnie Duka/Getty Images;
Page 8: Photodisc Collection/Getty Images; Page 10: Peter
Cade/Getty Images; Page 12: Siede Preis/Getty Images; Page
13: Teens in red car, Doug Menuez/Getty Images; Car in snow,
Mike Magnuson/Getty Images; Page 14: Spike Mafford/Getty
Images; Page 15: Romilly Lockyer; Page 16: Roger
Wright/Getty Images; Page 17: Milton Montenegro/Getty
Images; Page 18: William A. Allard/Getty Images; Page 20:
Adrian Weinbrecht/Getty Images; Page 22: ArtToday;
Page 23: Steve Schultz; Page 24: ArtToday; Page 26: SW
Productions/Getty Images; Page 29: Marc Romanelli/Getty
Images; Page 30: Digital Vision/Getty Images; Page 31: Megan
Stine; Page 32: Arthur Tilley/Getty Images; Page 35: Gislain
and Marie David de Lossy/Getty Images; Page 36: ArtToday;
Page 37: Ryan McVay/Getty Images; Page 38: Deborah
Jaffe/Getty Images; Page 40: Ryan McVay/Getty Images; Page
41: Benelux Press/Getty Images; Page 42: ArtToday; Page 45:
Megan Stine; Page 46: ArtToday; Page 47: Spike
Mafford/Getty Images; Page 48: Stewart Cohen/Getty Images;
Page 50: Megan Stine; Page 51: SW Productions/Getty Images;
Page 53: Digital Vision/Getty Images; Page 54: Roger
Wright/Getty Images; Page 55: PNC/Getty Images; Page 56:
Marc Romanelli/Getty Images; Page 57: Christian
Michaels/Getty Images; Page 58: Tomi/Photolink/Getty Images;
Page 60: Empty pockets, ArtToday; Man looking in window,
Adrian Weinbrecht/Getty Images; Page 62: Megan Stine;
Page 63: Tony Hopewell/Getty Images.

# realU

## GUIDE TO

# BUYING YOUR FIRST CAR

## JOHANNA BODNYK

# Your friends are sick of giving you rides...

You need some wheels of your own. Sure, your uncle Murray offered to sell you his '87 station wagon for a song, but you had something a little hipper in mind. Too bad negotiating for a car sounds like about as much fun as having root canal, and the biggest loan you ever took out was for a snack from the vending machine.

Lucky for you, Real U is here to help. Read on for the lowdown on picking the perfect new or used car, negotiating the lowest price, leasing, financing, and everything else you need to know about buying your first car.

But letting your uncle Murray down easy? That's your problem.

And welcome to real U

# GUIDE TO YOUR FIRST CAR
# TABLE OF CONTENTS

# ARE YOU A SAVVY BUYER OR A SUCKER?

Are you the kind of customer car salesmen dream about, or a savvy buyer who can bring even the best salesman to his knees with your awe-inspiring negotiation skills? Are you looking forward to the car buying process as a kill-or-be-killed challenge, or as a painful ordeal to be dealt with quickly and with the least amount of eye contact? Take this quiz to see where you score on the Car Buying Savvy-O-Meter.

*Have I got a deal for you!*

# 1.

You've been planning to buy a car for a while, and you think you're almost ready now. Your best friend asks what kind of car you're thinking of buying. You answer:

**A.** "Red. Definitely something red. Red, with a sunroof."

**B.** "I'd like it to get good mileage, and I guess it should be fairly cheap. I'm thinking of an SUV, you know?"

**C.** "Well, I've got it narrowed down to ten, and I've categorized them by size, gas mileage, safety rating, price range, color, smell, emotional assocations, and—here, this'll be easier to follow if I show you the spreadsheet and slide show..."

# 2.

You're at the dealership when a salesperson sidles up and asks, "So, what do you think of this one?" Your response is...

**A.** "Oh my God. I love this car. I must have this car. How much is it?"

**B.** "Well, it is pretty much exactly what I wanted. I'll bet these are pretty popular, huh?"

**C.** "Gee, I'm not sure. It's cute, but then again, so are golf carts."

*more quiz &
your grade* →

## 3.

After settling on a price, you arrive in the dealership's Finance and Insurance (F&I) office to wrap things up. The nice man behind the desk strongly recommends you invest in the dealer's Ultra Super Deluxe Stainproofing Fabric Protection. You reply...

**A.** "Wow, they make that? I am such a klutz! Sign me up for two."

**B.** "Uh, well, I hadn't really thought about it. I don't know, do you recommend it?"

**C.** "No. Nein. Nyet. Non. No thank you. Huh-uh."

## 4.

**Your car maintenance philosophy goes like this:**

**A.** Cars just need gas, and they'll tell you if anything goes wrong. That's what those little lights are for— although you tend to wait for the hood to start smoking so you know it's not a false alarm.

**B.** You know you should check your oil, but it's scary under there. What if you break something?

**C.** Let's just say the Owner's Manual is your bible. You sleep with it under your pillow, and you're in the process of writing a companion piece called "The Rhythm of the Car: Living My Life According to my Vehicle's Service Schedule."

*He sleeps with his owner's manual*

## 5.

You know your credit score probably isn't so hot. You've only had a credit card for a year, and there have been a couple nasty mall-related incidents. How do you handle the credit situation?

**A.** Head straight for the dealership and beg them to do their best. The guy offers you a monthly payment that sounds pretty good. Turns out it's actually a lease, but what's the difference, really?

**B.** Apply for a loan at your credit union, and after being turned down, sign up for First Time Buyer financing at a local dealership. The payments are straining your budget, and you have to pawn your grandmother's wedding ring to come up with the huge down payment, but at least you have a car.

**C.** Apply for financing everywhere you can think of. A few loan officers laugh in your face and call security, but you eventually get a reasonable rate, and then get the dealership to beat it.

# ANSWERS:

## MOSTLY A's

Wow. Can we sell you a car? We've got a red one you'll love. But seriously, you need a little help with the car buying process. Don't go near a car dealership until you've read at least half of this book—preferably not by reading every other word.

## MOSTLY B's

Your heart's in the right place, but most car salespeople aim a little lower. This guide will give you the confidence and knowledge you need to make the firm decisions that result in good deals.

## MOSTLY C's

You've got unemotional decision-making skills and unwavering willpower. We're a little afraid of you. But read on and we bet you'll find some advice even you didn't think of.

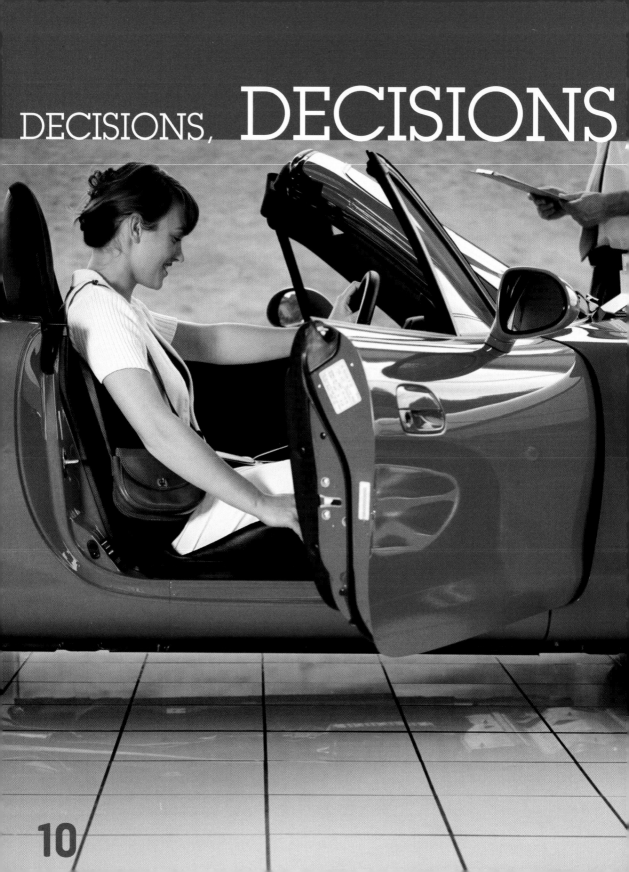

DECISIONS, **DECISIONS**

# DECISIONS

Remember when you wanted a pony more than anything in the whole wide world? Remember how your mom said "No," and then came up with something cold and logical about the fact that you lived in an apartment building? Well, the pony dream may be history now, but you're still lusting after something with a little horsepower.

All the same, fitting the sporty little car you've been craving into your budget—or stuffing that bruiser of an SUV into your parking space—might be about as easy as coaxing a pony into the elevator.

So before you go shopping, you've got to answer these basic questions:

- What type of vehicle is right for your needs?
- Do you want to buy new or used?
- What features do you really care about?
- Do you want things like safety, fuel efficiency, and reliability, or are you all about the sunroof and the sub-woofer?

- Which options do you need/crave? We're talking ABS, 4WD, LX, DX, EX, and lots of other abbreviations, here.
- What can you afford to buy?
- What can you afford to own?

It's a lot to think about, but in this chapter we're going to address these questions one by one, so you can understand all your options and find the perfect "pony," or "car," if you want to be cold and literal like your mother.

11

# WHAT TYPE OF VEHICLE IS RIGHT FOR YOUR NEEDS?

**Or, to put it differently, what are you going to do with your car? O.K., yes, you're going to drive it. Very funny. But where are you going to drive it, and who and what are you going to put into it?**

If you chauffeur your ten closest friends to the mall or the hockey rink all the time, that two-seater might be a little too cramped. And if parking is at a premium in your neighborhood, that mammoth SUV you're drooling over might be a huge and hairy mistake. Take a look at this list and check off any statement that rings true or close to true.

☐ I've got a three-hour commute to work or school in heavy, stop-and-go traffic. (Try a fuel efficient car with an automatic transmission…and maybe a nice sound system.)

☐ I regularly drive long distances in my job as a traveling encyclopedia salesperson. (You'll probably want a mid-sized sedan with good gas mileage, a big trunk, and a comfy ride.)

☐ I'm a sculptor who works in marble and bronze, and I transport my pieces myself—this motorcycle just isn't cutting it anymore! (A hatchback would be just the thing.)

☐ Sometimes I feel like I've got designated driver tattooed on my forehead. My friends, conveniently, are carless. (You need a roomy four door, five seat sedan, or maybe even a minivan.)

☐ My house is located in the middle of a swamp, and the driveway is unpaved. Also, it snows for half the year and it's hard to plow frozen swamp. (A rugged SUV with four-wheel drive or all-wheel drive can handle all that dangerous terrain.)

☐ My neighbors have started stacking their cars on top of each other to save space. Did I mention there isn't much parking here? (A teeny-tiny subcompact will fit in anywhere.)

☐ On a regular weekend, I tow my boat to the local lake, help a friend move her anvil collection, and drag huge trees I've felled from the tract of land I'm clearing for my homestead. Then on Sunday, I transport elephants for the circus. (A pickup truck with a towing package is a must.)

☐ I live in the flat flat desert, where the speed limit is 85...or is it 95? I can't remember—there are no speed limit signs on my way to work. (You need a car with a manual transmission and a big powerful engine!)

i should have gotten 4WD!

# NEW OR USED?

Ah, the eternal question: new or used? If you buy used, you can afford more for your money…but new cars are so shiny and pretty! Here are some pros and cons on both sides of the story to help you decide.

|  | NEW | USED |
|---|---|---|
| **PROS** | • Your car is in pristine condition<br><br>• It's under full warranty<br><br>• You get to choose the options you want<br><br>• Interest rates are typically lower<br><br>• You get brand-new technology, including better safety features in some cases<br><br>• That new car smell…and did we mention that it's shiny and pretty? | • A 3- or 4-year-old car is 40 to 60% cheaper than the same car new!<br><br>• Insurance and tag fees are cheaper<br><br>• You won't mind as much if you get a scratch |
| **CONS** | • It will cost more to buy… a lot more.<br><br>• Insurance and tag fees are more expensive | • It's harder to find the exact car you want<br><br>• Your car's past is a mystery— you just never know<br><br>• It's probably not as reliable<br><br>• It's not necessarily under warranty<br><br>• Interest rates for loans are higher |

John's USED CARS INC.

# WHAT FEATURES

## DO YOU REALLY CARE ABOUT?

**IS IT MORE IMPORTANT TO BE SUPER-SAFE, OR SUPER-STYLISH? DO YOU NEED, DEEP DOWN, TO BE ABLE DO ZERO TO SIXTY IN 7 SECONDS, OR WILL YOU SLEEP BETTER KNOWING THAT YOUR CAR IS FUEL EFFICIENT? DECISIONS, DECISIONS.**

## safety

Car crashes are the leading cause of death for all people ages 2 to 33. (That probably includes you, right?) Luckily, some cars are safer than others, but you'll have to make a few sacrifices if you want to put safety first.

**Features to look for:**
Active features include anti-lock brakes, traction control, electronic stability control, 4WD or AWD, superior visibility, and good tires. Passive safety features are things like airbags, head restraints, and a soundly constructed vehicle. The size of a car also affects the safety of its passengers. All other things being equal, larger cars are safer in a crash than smaller cars. But smaller cars are generally easier to steer and stop, which helps you avoid crashes in the first place.

**How to find out:**
The government conducts crash tests, and so does the insurance industry. To find out which cars are safest in an accident, go to www.realuguides.com and click on Buying Your First Car for links.

**Trade-offs:**
Safety features are expensive. However, since safer cars tend to cost less to insure, you could end up making some of that money back. If you choose the safety of a larger vehicle, you'll lose out on the fuel economy of smaller cars.

# reliability

Choosing a reliable car can save you lots of money—not to mention the major hassle of going into the shop for frequent repairs and having to sell your kidney to pay for them. Keep your bodily organs for your own use.

## Features to look for:

If reliability is important to you, you'll want to choose a car that's known for needing few repairs. Don't assume that a car with a great reputation is still a top choice, however. Reliability can vary from one model year to another, especially when the manufacturer redesigns the car, so you'll have to do some research.

## How to find out:

Consumer Reports publishes an annual car buyer's guide each spring, with reliability ratings. For additional rating information, go to www.realuguides.com. Also talk to friends who own the kind of car you are considering.

## Trade-offs:

The reliability of a well-made car might cost you more in the beginning, but if you spend less on repairs you can still come out on top.

*sixth time this month!*

# fuel economy

If only cars would run on pixie dust and happy thoughts. Oh, if only. Back to reality: Cars run on gasoline, and some of them run on much more gasoline than others. Some examples: Honda's tiny two-seat hybrid Insight gets an amazing 66 highway miles per gallon. Lamborghini's Mucielago gets 13 mpg. An average fuel-efficient small car gets around 37 mpg, while a typical SUV gets only 15 mpg. Why should you care? Two reasons. First, motor vehicles cause 50% of all air pollution. The more gas you use, the more you pollute. Second, gas costs money. If you drive 15,000 miles in a year and pay $1.50 a gallon for gas, you'll only spend $567 a year on gas for that efficient small car. Gassing the large SUV will run more than twice as much, at $1401. Just think what you can buy with that extra $834!

## Features to look for:

Obviously, smaller cars and smaller engines get the best mileage. Other features that help are manual transmissions and diesel engines.

## How to find out:

Compare gas mileage on cars and check out the best and worst of the crop at www.realuguides.com

## Trade-offs:

Smaller cars use less gas, but bigger cars are safer, especially if you tend to follow people closely or drive 60 mph in snowstorms.

## How to Save Big Bucks on Gas: Hybrid Electric Vehicles

No, they don't fly. But at 50 mpg, who needs to fly? Hybrid electric vehicles (HEV's) run on an energy-efficient combination of gasoline and electricity. A small gasoline-powered engine gets things going and does the driving at high speeds, while the battery-powered electric motor helps out with hills and acceleration, and takes over at low speeds. When the car is coasting or braking, the engine acts as a generator and recharges the battery. So, unlike fully electric cars, HEV's never need to be plugged in.

Unfortunately, HEV's are expensive. The price tag can be $3,500 to $6,000 more than a regular car. Though you'll save on gasoline, it'll take a while to make up the difference there. The snazzy batteries in these babies are also a little pricey—$3,000 to $8,000—though they are usually under warranty for at least 80,000 miles. And since HEV's are pretty much brand new, you'll have a tough time buying one used. One plus: The federal government is offering nice tax breaks for buyers of HEV's through 2006. Check out www.realuguides.com for more info.

# power, performance, and handling

**EAT MY DUST!**

Any car you buy is gonna go, stop, and turn. We hope. Performance is a measure of how well it does these things. A car with good power accelerates smoothly and quickly, giving you the extra oomph necessary to perform death-defying feats like merging in front of a speeding tractor-trailer. Whee! If you change your mind at the last second (as you probably should) good brakes will let you slow down quickly on the entrance ramp.

## Features to look for:
Performance depends largely on the size of the engine (a big engine means more power) and the mechanical quality of the car. Anti-lock brakes, traction control and electronic stability control improve handling on slippery roads.

## How to find out:
Pick up one of the latest car magazines or buyer's guides. Edmunds.com also conducts road tests and write reviews of new vehicles, rating them on performance.

## Trade-offs:
If you want the power a big engine provides, you'll have to sacrifice some fuel economy. You'll also pay higher insurance premiums for a higher performance car.

# cost

You don't want to break the bank on your first car, but the used car you buy sight unseen for $200 bucks probably doesn't even have doors. Or wheels. Or an engine. On the other hand, you may get a great deal on a new car, but you won't save any money if you're constantly in the shop, or you're filling the tank every 20 miles. Bottom line: You get what you pay for.

## Features to look for:
The fewer options you add on, the less expensive your new ride will be. But don't sacrifice the things you really need, or you might end up wanting to buy a whole new car before the ink on your financing agreement is dry.

## How to find out:
The websites of individual car manufacturers list the Manufacturer's Suggested Retail Price (MSRP) of the cars they sell. You won't have to pay this much (we hope), but it can help you figure out some ballpark prices. Also, Consumers Reports offers a quick look at the dealer's invoice for all options available on each car. For links to websites that can help you calculate the cost of ownership, visit www.realuguides.com.

## Trade-offs:
For a super-cheap car you'll probably have to compromise on just about everything. You'll at least need to kiss the leather seats goodbye.

# MINIVANS AND SUV'S

If you're thinking about a car that's big enough to haul your drum kit or roomy enough to sleep in when you're camping in Yellowstone, you're probably choosing between a minivan and an SUV. Both offer increased cargo space, and both give you that reassuring, all-powerful sense of looking down on other cars from high above. But there are some big differences between the two. For one, minivans tend to handle like cars, while SUV's handle like trucks, and are harder to steer and stop. For another, since SUV's are built on a truck base, the ride isn't nearly as comfortable as in a car or minivan. Nevertheless, SUV's are so popular right now that even the most die-hard environmentalist probably wonders somewhere deep down whether she'd look kinda cool driving one. But before you join the SUV craze, you should know the other, not-so-cool, side of the story.

### Bad for your budget
Not only do SUV's have a higher sticker price than cars, they also cost more to register and insure.

### Poor fuel economy
SUV's are major gas guzzlers. The average SUV gets only 15 miles per gallon, and that extra fuel is harmful to the environment.

### Safety
Rollovers, or accidents in which a vehicle flips over, are the deadliest type of car crash. In 2001, rollovers caused 33% of all crash-related fatalities. SUV's are more than twice as likely to roll over than regular cars. Although most car crashes aren't the rollover variety, a high percentage of accidents involving teenage drivers are rollovers. And in other crashes, the passengers of regular cars hit by SUV's are 6 times more likely to die than if they'd been hit by another car. Ouch.

# WHICH OPTIONS DO YOU NEED/CRAVE?

## Just when you thought you'd made all the hard choices, here are a few more options to consider.

### Manual vs. Automatic Transmission

Manual transmissions improve your gas mileage a little and have slightly better acceleration. Plus you get to show off 'cause you know how to drive a stick. If, of course, you don't know how to drive a stick shift, it can be tricky to learn. Manuals also tend to be cheaper, at least when they are "standard" equipment. On the other hand, automatics are now standard in most models, and they're a blessing in city driving and heavy traffic.

### 4, 6, or 8 cylinders

Though a bigger engine will cost more and use more gas, it definitely has advantages. Six or eight cylinders are quieter and more durable than four. They also give you better acceleration and a smoother ride.

### Antilock Brakes

ABS keeps you from skidding and losing control when you slam on the brakes. How? The antilock braking system senses when a wheel locks up and adjusts the breaks automatically. This allows you to concentrate on not crashing into that snowplow.

# THOUGH A BIGGER ENGINE WILL COST MORE AND USE MORE GAS, IT DEFINITELY HAS ADVANTAGES.

## Traction Control

Traction control uses the same technology as ABS but does the opposite thing—it senses when a wheel is spinning uselessly and applies the brakes till you regain traction.

## 4WD, AWD, NoWD

O.K., that last one isn't really an option—we just wanted to see if you were still paying attention. Most cars are front-wheel drive, meaning the engine turns the wheels up front, while the ones in the back just roll along behind. Front wheel drive provides good traction, and is adequate in most conditions. Rear wheel drive, which used to be standard, is now only used for sports cars and pickup trucks. Though rear wheel drive vehicles corner and brake well on dry surfaces, they can be really bad news in the rain or snow. Four wheel drive (4WD) and all wheel drive (AWD) sound like they should be the same thing, but that would be too easy! Both are good in snow and mud and other tractionless surfaces, but 4WD does a little better. The problem is that 4WD shouldn't be driven on dry pavement, so you have to turn it off and on. Since AWD can handle any surface at any time, it's always on, which means it's there to save your butt when you hit an unexpected patch of ice.

## Electronic Stability Control

This feature helps you turn the car in low traction situations. When you lose traction in a curve it's easy to under- or over-steer, and end up on the side of the road wrapped around a tree. ESC uses ABS technology, a computer, and sensors—or as we like to call it, magic—to figure out where your car is supposed to be going when it's turning too sharply or shallowly. Then it takes over and applies brakes to an individual wheel, basically steering for you until the crisis is over. Huzzah!

## Variable Ride Height Suspension

Haven't you always wanted to press a button and make your car go up and down, like one of those crazy monster trucks? Actually a safety feature rather than a toy, variable ride height suspension allows SUV's to be lowered when driving around town and on highways, and raised when you're driving over rough, unpaved terrain, or the front lawns of your enemies. With a lower ride, the center of gravity isn't as high and the SUV is less likely to flip over.

## Airbags

Front-impact airbags are standard equipment on almost all new cars, but they don't protect you from side impacts. You'll want side-impact airbags for that. Some side-impact airbags also work as rollover protection to keep you from being ejected if your SUV flips over.

*I had to have it.*

# What can you afford to buy?

So you've picked out the perfect car—great! Can you really afford those monthly payments? Here are 2 rules to help you think about how much to shell out for car payments each month:

## RULE 1

Your car payment should probably equal no more than 20% of your monthly paycheck. Bye-bye, Porsche!

## RULE 2

You don't want to finance for more than 4 years. Why? Because a 5-year loan can put you at risk of owing more for your car than it's worth—so if it's wrecked or stolen, you're in deep trouble. See Driving Upside Down on Page 50 for more on this situation.

BUYING A 2-YEAR-OLD CAR THAT'S STILL UNDER WARRANTY CAN SAVE YOU THOUSANDS.

# What can you afford to own?

**There are all kinds of wallet-draining expenses associated with owning a set of wheels. Don't be forced to charge your friends for rides. Take this stuff into account when you're budgeting for a car.**

### TAXES AND FEES
When you buy your car, the taxes and fees can be as high as 10% of the price you've negotiated!

### INSURANCE
Car insurance on a $20,000 vehicle can cost from $400 to $2000 a year. The kind of car you drive and the options it has both affect the price of your insurance. Certain safety features lower your rates. For more on the variables that affect your insurance rates, check out How to Lower Your Premiums on Page 59.

### GAS
Your car won't do you much good if you don't put gas in it. If you drive 15,000 miles a year in a car that gets 30 miles per gallon (mpg), and gas costs 1.50 a gallon, fuel is gonna run you $750 annually. If you get fewer mpg, gas will cost even more.

### MAINTENANCE AND REPAIRS
Between oil changes, tune-ups, new tires and repairs, keeping your car in good shape can add up to anything from $200 to $1,000+ a year.

### PARKING, TOLLS, TICKETS
If you regularly feed a meter, take a toll road, or get caught speeding, be sure to add these figures to your car costs.

# THE COST OF OWNERSHIP

The sticker price of a new car is only one factor to consider in figuring costs. Check out this chart which compares the cost of owning a 2004 Honda Civic and a 2004 Ford Mustang for a period of 5 years. Figures have been rounded.

## 2004 HONDA CIVIC

## 2004 FORD MUSTANG

**STICKER PRICE**

 $15,000

 $25,000

**FUEL**

**REPAIRS & MAINTENANCE**

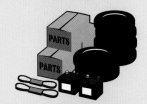

**INTEREST, INSURANCE, AND TAXES OR TAG FEES**

**DEPRECIATION**

**TOTAL COST OF OWNERSHIP**

 $22,000

 $38,000

It's easy to negotiate if you
understand the rules of the game

# BUYING A NEW CAR

Buying a new car doesn't have to be a nerve-wracking nail-biting whirlwind of confusion. If you take your time, do your homework, and don't let yourself be pressured, you'll have all the ammunition you need to combat the salespeople. Here are ten easy steps to buying a new car.

## STEP ONE

### Do Your Homework

If you read the first chapter, you've already done a fair amount of research. If you didn't read it, you're getting ahead of yourself, buddy. Go back and study up.

Once you've figured out options and thought about what you can afford, you'll want to research the specific cars you're interested in. Let's say you like the Subaru Outback, but you're also lusting after the VW Beetle convertible. Great—you've narrowed it down to two. Before you even think of walking into a dealership, go online and get more info about each car.

*9 more steps to go!* →

27

# STEP TWO
## Visit Dealerships

You can learn an amazing amount without ever changing out of your PJ's, but there's no substitute for meeting a car in real life. Put on some pants and get out there! Note the sticker prices and find out how comfy the seats are. But remember that you definitely aren't ready to buy yet. Think of this as a first date—it's always a bad idea to go too far too fast. If you know you can't be trusted, bring a friend along as a chaperone.

# STEP THREE
## Take Test Drives

To get the most out of your test drive, ask to leave the salesperson behind, so you can concentrate on the car without someone yammering at you. Once you've pried the keys from his death-grip and are cruising down the road, ask yourself these questions:

- Is the ride comfortable, smooth and quiet?
- Does the car accelerate powerfully and brake smoothly?
- Do you feel like you are in control of the steering? Does the car respond well?
- Are the seats comfortable? Do they adjust to fit you?
- Is the steering wheel a good fit? Does it adjust?
- Can you easily reach all the controls, or do you have to put your head below the dashboard to see the radio knob?

- Can you see well? Visibility—through the front, back, and side windows, and in all the mirrors—is an important safety feature.
- How about the cupholders? Never underestimate the importance of good cupholders!
- Make sure to take the car onto the highway so you can really test its performance at higher speeds.

As you test drive cars, you can also evaluate the dealership and its salespeople, to decide if it's worth coming back. But remember, you are still not buying a car today…it's only the second date!

# STEP FOUR
## Line Up Financing

This is probably the most important car-buying rule: Never go into the dealership to buy a car until you've lined up your own financing. Although dealerships can sometimes offer good financing, especially for first-time buyers, shopping around for financing options and getting pre-approved before you go to buy has several benefits. First, you know which cars you can reasonably afford. Second, you can negotiate on price more powerfully if you know you've got the "cash" to back you up. And third, if you've shopped around for financing, you'll know whether the dealership is offering you a better deal. For more info on financing, see Page 49.

# STEP FIVE

## Locate The Car You Want To Buy

If you spotted the exact red and black Mini Cooper you want in the research phase, great! But don't stop there. Check with other dealerships, too. The more dealerships that have the car you want, the stronger your bargaining position will be. You can do this by e-mailing, calling or faxing local dealerships.

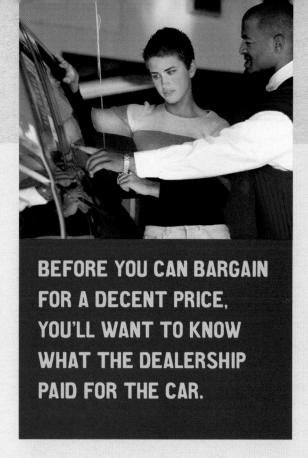

**BEFORE YOU CAN BARGAIN FOR A DECENT PRICE, YOU'LL WANT TO KNOW WHAT THE DEALERSHIP PAID FOR THE CAR.**

# STEP SIX

## Do More Homework

You're almost to the buying stage…but first, a little more research. Before you can bargain for a decent price on your new car, you'll want to know what the dealership paid for it. (For some reason, dealers don't tend to advertise this information.) The factory invoice price is what the dealership literally paid for the car—but that's not the end of the story. Manufacturers give dealer rebates (also known as "factory-to-dealer cash") to help the dealers sell slow-moving cars. (That would be cars that aren't selling well, not cars that don't drive very fast.) If a dealer shells out $18,000 for a car, but gets $1,000 back right away, they really only paid $17,000 for the car, right? Of course they want to keep that $1,000 as part of their profit. But if you know about it, you can grab some of it as part of your savings.

To find out all about invoice prices and dealer incentives, go online to Edmunds.com, kbb.com, and FightingChance.com. Sometimes manufacturers will also offer incentives to you. You can save up to a couple thousand if you buy when the car you want is on "sale," so keep track of the incentives being offered. You might be offered a rebate or financing at a low APR—but usually not both. Zero percent financing might sound like the best deal, but the rebate might actually save you more since it means you have less to finance. Edmunds.com provides a calculator to help you crunch those numbers. If you choose the rebate, make sure they deduct it from the purchase price of the car. (You don't want to wait for your cash back, do you?)

**NEVER TALK ABOUT FINANCING WITH A DEALER UNTIL YOU'VE NEGOTIATED THE PRICE.**

# STEP EIGHT

## Negotiate Financing and (if necessary) Your Trade-In

Here comes another major rule: Never talk about financing or trade-ins with a dealer until you've negotiated the price of the new car. In fact, the best plan is to get pre-approved for financing from somewhere else, before you hit the dealership. That way, you'll know if the dealership's financing offer is reasonable. Ditto for trading in your old car. Do the research first so you know what it's worth. Or even better, sell your old car privately, since you'll never get as much in a trade-in as you will if you sell it yourself.

# STEP NINE

## Close the Deal

When it's time to sign the paperwork, you'll be led into a life-sized trap called the "back room"—the den of the Finance and Insurance (F&I) manager. This is where the Finance Manager will try to convince you that without $200 upholstery protection, your car is barely going to run and will most likely burst into flames. Repeat after us: Just say no to add-ons. Items like undercoating and VIN etching are over-priced, usually unnecessary, and just there to earn the dealership more profit. Extended warranties are sometimes a good idea, but they can be purchased much more cheaply. See Page 37 for more about warranties.

# STEP SEVEN

## Negotiate The Price

Okay, the moment of truth. Excited? Nervous? Hiding under a table? Hey—it's easy to negotiate if you understand the rules of the game. Check out the Rules of Negotiation on Page 34, and take a peek at Know Your Enemy on Page 32 as well.

# STEP TEN

## Take Delivery

When you pick up your car, you need to take a good long look at it before you drive away. Thoroughly inspect the car inside and out, and make sure it has all the optional equipment you were expecting. If anything is wrong, now is the time to demand that it be fixed. If it's been a while since you test-drove the car, you might want to do it again, just to be extra safe.

# All About the Contract

When you're signing the contract, you may notice a lot of add-on fees. Some of them are:

- Freight or transportation. This should be included in the dealer invoice. Ask to see it, so you don't get charged twice.

- Dealer prep. Ditto.

- ADM (additional dealer markup), ADP (additional dealer profit), and MVA (market value adjustment). These basically translate into "give us more money just because we said so." Try to contest them, or find a dealer who doesn't add them. As a basic guideline, assume that charges printed on the contract are likely to stay there, while anything written in afterwards is easier to have canceled.

Take your time when reviewing the contract, and don't assume it's all over your head. Once you've signed, the car is yours—there is no cooling-off period for car purchases. Here are some tips to make sure the contract reflects the deal you made:

- Check all the numbers and make sure they jibe with what you negotiated.

- Be sure that the options you want, and nothing extra, are listed.

- Read every word before you sign. Pay close attention to the small print, since that's where it's easy to hide stuff.

- If you don't understand something, ask what it means. It's not your fault they make it so confusing!

- Cross out all blank spaces and get all changes initialed by the dealership.

- Get all agreements in writing. Verbal promises are worthless.

# Know Your Enemy

## All About Dealerships

### The Game

From the dealership's point of view, the object of the game is simple: (1) Sell you a car today, and (2) Make as much profit as possible doing so. The now-or-never mind-set accounts for why they'll do everything short of chaining you down to keep you from walking out the door. As for making as much profit as possible, this doesn't necessarily mean charging you more for the car. They also count on other aspects of the deal, like the financing, your trade-in, and add-ons to contribute to their profit. This is why the salesperson wants to know right away how you plan to pay for the car and what you're going to do with your old one. Don't tell them.

### The Tactics and Tricks

Some of these tricks are what all dealers do to make a semi-honest buck. But some of these tricks are a little sketchier, or even illegal. A good way to avoid getting seriously scammed is to investigate dealerships before you visit them. Ask around, and call your local Better Business Bureau to see if anyone has made complaints.

### Your Friend the Salesperson

Just because you don't see horns and a pitchfork, don't assume a car salesperson is on your side. She may be friendly and sympathetic, and promise to "see what she can do" when she takes your offer to the sales manager, but there's one thing you must never forget: she works on commission, which means the more you pay, the more she makes.

### The Siege

This is where salespeople try to keep you at the dealership for so long that you buy a car out of desperation and hunger. They'll go away for half an hour at a time, "considering your offer," or "taking a meeting," or "picking up their dry-cleaning." You can either threaten to leave, or come prepared to wait them out. Bring a tent and a sleeping bag—that ought to throw 'em.

### The Lowball Offer

If you get a really low offer right away, be suspicious. It's probably bogus. If you got the offer over the phone, the salesperson is just trying to get you into the dealership, and will likely never give you that price.

If you have a solid understanding of how car dealerships function, you'll be able to see through all the mind games and even play a few of your own.

## Pressure Tactics

Since they want you to buy now, salespeople will try to pressure you into signing by claiming a price is only good today. Umm, why? Is it based on the phases of the moon? Unless they can give you a good reason, this is nonsense. If you want to buy the car tomorrow, they're not going to refuse to sell it to you.

## "We don't negotiate"

Wait, what? Oh, I thought this was a car dealership. I guess you're just here to sell lemonade. Gee, my mistake, I'll go somewhere else. There are "no-dicker" dealerships, where they really don't negotiate, but these are definitely advertised as such.

## Backing Out

A salesperson might agree on a low price, get you ready to finalize things, and then come back all sheepish-like saying the sales manager wouldn't go for it. This is irritating, since you've spent a lot of time to get this far, but the last thing you should do is give in and pay more because you're tired of it all. Best plan: Leave and try another dealership.

## The Deposit Check

Some dealerships ask you to write a deposit check when you make an offer so they'll know you're serious about it. What, are you just out negotiating car deals to kill some time on a slow afternoon? If you write them a check, it's harder to make good on your threats to walk out the door. Don't do it.

## The Credit Check

If a salesperson asks for your birth date and Social Security number before the financing stage, don't give it to him. Dealerships like to run credit checks on potential customers to see if they are able to pay, and how much they are able to pay. You don't want them to have this information about you. You also don't want unnecessary inquiries on your credit report, because that hurts your credit score. It's illegal for a dealership to run a credit check on you without your permission before you agree to buy. Don't give them permission.

# 10 RULES OF NEGOTIATION

## 1. FIND THE BEST PRICE

The easiest and most relaxed way is to do it all by telephone. Call dealerships who have your car, let them know you are shopping around for the best price, and ask for their lowest offer. Then take the best offer you get, call the other dealers back, and see if they can beat that price. Repeat this process until you've gone as low as you can. You might also be able to play this game with the Internet, or using e-mail to solicit quotes.

Some dealerships won't give you prices over the phone. They'll require that you come in to talk to them. You might be able to negotiate a better price this way, so give it a try—it'll put hair on your chest. But don't even think about walking into a dealership and talking price until you've read the rest of these rules.

When you've negotiated a price and you think the dealer has gone as low as they're willing to go, it's a good idea to leave and tell him you want to sleep on it for a day. You might be surprised to find out that the price drops again! And if it doesn't, you can always go back tomorrow to buy the car at the negotiated price.

## 2. MAKE IT CLEAR YOU MEAN BUSINESS

The salesperson needs to know that you are a qualified buyer ready to hand over some cash in exchange for a new ride. If you act like you know what you're doing, you're less likely to get pushed around.

## 3. BE COOL

Don't let them see how much you want the car, or you'll end up paying more. Your attitude should say "I kind of like that car, but then again I've been thinking of commuting by horse and buggy, so…."

## 4. BE PREPARED TO WALK AWAY

This is important for two reasons. First, if you are being pressured or bullied, or you just don't feel comfortable, you need to get out of there before you cave in to a bad deal. Second, your readiness to leave is a key negotiating tool, because it's the very last thing a salesperson wants you to do. Gathering your things and heading for the door often works to magically generate lower offers.

## 5. TAKE YOUR TIME

Car negotiations can be a drawn out process, and the last thing you need is to put pressure on yourself. So don't head out to bargain for a car when you've got a hot date in two hours, or when you're hungry or tired.

## 6. DON'T BE AFRAID TO MAKE A REALLY LOW OFFER

What's the worst that could happen? They laugh in your face and then call in other customers to laugh too? No, the worst that could happen is that you offer too much, pay more than you need to, and they laugh behind your back while they count your money.

## 7. NEVER TALK ABOUT FINANCING OR TRADE-INS UNTIL YOU'VE SETTLED ON PRICE

A salesperson can give you a low price on your new car and still make big money if you finance with the dealership and trade in your car. Naturally then, he wants to know up front if you're going to do those things. Play it cool. Let him think it's a possibility, but don't talk about specifics. Politely insist that you don't want to discuss financing and your trade-in till you've agreed on a price.

## 8. DON'T NEGOTIATE IN TERMS OF MONTHLY PAYMENTS

Salespeople will often try to convince you that they're offering you a good deal by talking about monthly payments—$275, for instance.Forget that. You need to hear the dealer's "cash price" to know if you are getting a good deal.

## 9. LET THEM KNOW THEY ARE COMPETING FOR THE SALE

You'll get lower offers if the salesperson knows you might buy your car somewhere else.

## 10. BRING A FRIEND

The salesperson is not your friend, so bring someone who is. A parent is usually a safe bet, as is your level-headed best friend who refused to let you buy that amazing 10-in-1 slicer-dicer tool you saw on TV.

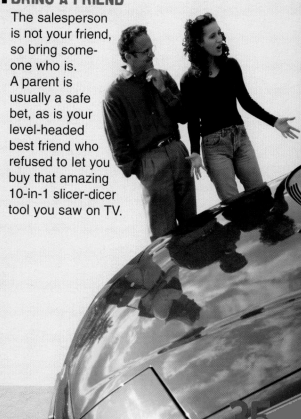

# If You Hate to Negotiate...

**Join the club. Few people really enjoy spending hours arguing over money, although you'll get the best deal if you do. But if you can't handle the negotiation thing, here are some alternatives.**

### NO-HAGGLE DEALERS

Saturn started it, and many private dealerships have followed in their footsteps. Why? Because they make more money that way! When you don't negotiate, you pay more for your car. Period.

### BUYING AND REFERRAL SERVICES

Buying services and referral services do most of their business online, which makes them super-convenient once you get over the fact that you're buying a car in cyberspace. Referral services operate by getting a "discount" quote from a dealer in their network. These services are free to the buyer—the services stay afloat by charging dealerships to be in their network. Although the quote you get might be reasonable, it isn't as low as it would be if you negotiated yourself. Buying services are typically fee-based, and chances are you'll pay a lot more for your car if you go this route.

### BROKERS

This is the same thing as a buying service, but offline and on an individual level. Some brokers really are on your side, but many are also taking commissions from dealerships, which is something of a conflict of interests. Generally, the more you pay them, the less they need to get from dealers, and the better your price will be. But whether you spend more money on a good broker or more money on a car because you chose a bad broker, you're still paying more than you really need to.

*bought my car online*

# Is This Piece Supposed to Fall Off?
# Warranties and Lemon Laws

All new cars come with warranties—some longer than others. But the real question is: What happens when the warranty runs out?

## EXTENDED WARRANTIES

Extended warranties take over when the basic warranty ends, and you pay extra for that. Should you buy one? That depends. If you are leasing a car or plan to sell it before the basic warranty runs out, an extended warranty is pointless. However, if you're buying a car that has a reputation for having mechanical problems and/or you plan to keep the car a long time, this option may well be worth your money. Extended warranties are sometimes marked up by as much as 100%, though, and guess what? The F&I guy works on commission. So remember: You don't have to buy the extended warranty when you buy the car, and you don't have to buy it from the same dealership where you bought the car. In most cases you have at least a month to decide. Shop around and talk to multiple F&I managers to find the best price. You should, however, always buy your warranty from the manufacturer. Independent companies that offer warranties can go out of business, leaving you out of luck.

## LEMON LAWS

All cars break down sooner or later. But some brand-new cars break down badly, right away, and defy all efforts at repair. These cars are lemons. Although lemon laws differ from state to state, the legal definition of a lemon is usually something like this:

- The car has a problem, covered by warranty, that has not been repaired after 4 attempts, or after a total of 30 days in the shop.

- The problem occurred within the first year or 12,000 miles.

- The problem wasn't caused by something dumb you did.

To protect your legal rights, make sure you keep good records. Save the receipts from all the repair attempts. If your warranty specifies that you need to tell the manufacturer about the recurring problem, be sure to do so, and document this as well. For a complete step-by-step on dealing with a lemon, go to www.realuguides.com. Bottom line: If your car is a lemon, the manufacturer has to give you a new one or refund your money. Yes!

# USED CAR

Yeah, you'll have to forego the new car smell and the general shininess, but if you buy a used car, at least you can brag to your friends that you saved some money.

## HERE ARE SEVEN STEPS TO BUYING A USED CAR:

## STEP ONE

**Sort out your priorities and do your homework.**

Besides four wheels and a steering wheel, what are you looking for? Do you absolutely have to have a blue Toyota hatchback with a great sound system, or do just need something under $3,000 that isn't going to explode? Are you willing to take a green car in excellent condition with low mileage—even if you hate green?

When it comes to shopping for a used car, flexibility is your new best friend. Remember that you'll lose a lot of bargaining power if there's only one car out there and you've gotta have it, no matter what.

# STEP TWO

### Line up financing.

What you do here depends on how much car you're buying. If you're getting a two-year-old "like new" number from a new car dealer, emptying your piggy bank isn't going to cut it. You'll need to finance your purchase, and it's wisest to shop around for financing before you go to buy. On the other hand, if you're buying a 10-year-old car, you might have a tough time finding a bank loan. (In that case, you may need to beg your grandma for a loan or save up until you can afford to pay cash.)

# STEP THREE

### Find your car(s).

There's pretty much only one way to find a new car—go to a dealership. But there are lots of different ways to find and buy used cars—so many that we wrote a whole section called "Used Car Hunting." Read more about it on Page 44.

Found the perfect car!

# STEP FOUR

## Size up your find.

Unless you like to live dangerously, you need to check out a used car very carefully before you buy. We're talking a thorough mechanical inspection here—and then some. Here are the steps to finding out just what's under the hood of that beast with four wheels.

• Order a Carfax report—a report which tells you whether a car has ever had a salvage title, been bought back as a lemon, or had it's odometer rolled back. For more on what all that means and why it's bad, see Page 47.

• Ask the seller for the car's maintenance records. If a car has been well-maintained, its life expectancy goes way up.

• You also need to see the car in person, size it up and take a test drive. You can find test driving tips on Page 28. Make sure you inspect the car in the daytime when all the flaws will show, not at night. Before paying a mechanic to inspect a car, there are few simple things you can look for yourself to see if it's worth your time and money. See How to Sniff Out a Stinker on Page 45.

• Having the car you want to buy inspected by an independent mechanic is absolutely vital. If a private owner resists letting you take the car to be inspected, you may be able to find a traveling mechanic who will come to the car. If the seller just doesn't want you to have it inspected at all, that's a red flag. Say goodbye.

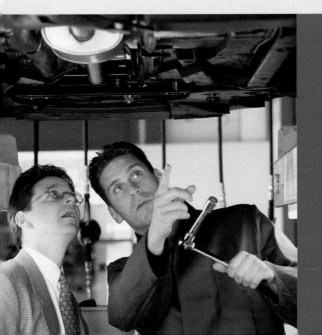

IF THE SELLER JUST DOESN'T WANT YOU TO HAVE IT INSPECTED AT ALL, THAT'S A RED FLAG. SAY GOODBYE.

# STEP FIVE

### Research price.

Knowing the value of the car you want to buy will be one of your most important negotiating tools. Unfortunately, the exact value of a used car is a very slippery thing. Since it's based on a bunch of variables like mileage, condition, popularity, geography, and how much the seller paid, the price of each used car is unique. But that doesn't mean you can't figure out a ballpark. Here's what to do: Get figures from all of the different publications that claim to have a handle on the true price of used cars. You can find the Kelley Blue Book, Edmunds, and the NADA Guide in your local library, or get prices online at www.kbb.com, www.edmunds.com, www.nadaguides.com, and www.carprice.com. Do some of your own pricing research by checking out how much similar cars are being offered for in the newspaper and on used car lots. Keep in mind that these are asking prices, not how much people are paying. Now average it all out, add a dash of common sense, and you'll have a good idea about price.

# STEP SIX

### Negotiate the best possible deal.

If you're buying your used car from a dealer, you can use most of the same tactics that new car buyers use. See the The Rules of Negotiation on Page 34.

Negotiating with a private party is a low-key affair—you don't have to worry about pressure tactics and high-priced add-ons, and you might be able to do it all over the phone. However, the basic negotiating rules like staying cool and starting low apply here too, and you can still save more money if you know what you're doing.

# BUYING USED: DEALERSHIP OR INDIVIDUAL?

| | INDIVIDUAL | DEALERSHIP |
|---|---|---|
| Price | Asking price is generally lower. | Higher markup. |
| Tax | No sales tax in many states. | Most states collect sales tax. |
| Warranty | For newer cars, remainder of manufacturer's warranty and extended warranties may be available | Some dealers provide small warranty to cover "unknown factors." Remainder of manufacturers warranty and extended warranties may be available. |
| Returns | Not available. | Some dealers offer limited return privileges. |
| Financing | Not available. | Yes—As an alternative to banks that may refuse a loan for older vehicles or for individuals with poor credit. |

# STEP SEVEN

**Wrap things up and take delivery.**

Again, if you're buying from a dealership, this part is pretty much just like buying a new car. Note that return policies are more common for used car purchases. If your dealer offers one, be sure to read it carefully and get any verbal promises in writing.

If you're buying from a private party the process is obviously a little different. The seller will most likely expect to be paid in cash or with a cashier's check, and will want to conduct the transaction at her bank or at the Department of Motor Vehicles. Make sure you receive the transferred title and a bill of sale listing both the buyer's and seller's names and addresses; the car's make, model, year, mileage, and VIN; and the amount and method of payment. For a downloadable contract you can use when buying or selling a used car, go to www.realugiudes.com. Get the vehicle registered in your name as soon as possible,and don't forget in some states that you owe a bit of sales tax. Your DMV can help fill in the details.

# Used Car Hunting: What to Look For (And What to Avoid)

### THE TWO-YEAR-OLD PREVIOUSLY LEASED CAR

A car in its terrific two's has already been hit with some of the worst depreciation, yet it still has a year to go before the warranty expires. That's good. Leased cars have usually been driven carefully and maintained regularly to avoid violating lease terms. Also good. Plus, since leases have mileage caps, a car sold after a lease expires will have relatively low mileage. Very good. You'll pay more for the benefits of buying this kind of car, but if you can afford it, that's, well, good.

### YOUR AUNT'S OLD CAR

Tied for first place with the two-year-old leased car is the car you buy from family or friends. Your aunt isn't going to try to make a ridiculous profit, and you can trust that she'll tell you everything she knows about it. Plus, you know what kind of driver she is, and how the car has been maintained. One warning: Although she'll tell you the stuff she knows about, she's not a mechanic. It's still your job to get the car inspected so a bad transmission doesn't ruin your next family reunion.

### FACTORY-CERTIFIED "PRE-OWNED" CARS

Many of the choicest used cars that are traded in or returned from a lease are inspected, fluffed up, and then sold as factory-certified used vehicles, often with brand-new warranties. Sure, these cars cost more, but the manufacturer stands behind the quality of the car, which is always nice. Manufacturer's programs differ, so be sure to get all the details on the one you are considering. Intellichoice.com rates different certification programs.

### DEMOS

Demonstration cars are models that have been driven by the dealer staff. They aren't exactly used, but they aren't brand new either. It's hard to pin down the right value for a demonstration car, but if a salesperson tries to tell you a demo is as good as new, don't believe it. These cars have real miles on them, and often their warranties have started running out. The price you pay should reflect this. On the upside, these cars have been well-maintained.

## eBAY

A lot of people are buying and selling cars on eBay (and other online auction sites) these days. In order to avoid the pitfalls of buying a car you've never seen from a person you've never met, follow these rules. First, only buy a car online from someone who lives close enough for you to go inspect it in person. Second, arrange to handle the financial transaction face to face. Otherwise, your online payment could go through at about th same time as the seller decides to take off for Canada.

## RENTAL CARS

Rental cars are the motel mattresses of the used car world—they've seen all kinds of action, some of it pretty frightening to contemplate. Although rental cars have been well-maintained and are often sold after one or two years, they have a lot of miles on them. More importantly, those miles have been put there by people who are never going to see the car again. Rental cars have been driven hard, and may give up the ghost much sooner than other used cars.

# HOW TO SNIFF OUT A STINKER

YOU KNOW YOU SHOULD HAVE A MECHANIC LOOK AT A USED CAR BEFORE YOU BUY IT. BUT FACE IT—INSPECTING EVERY CAR YOU COME ACROSS CAN GET PRETTY PRICEY PRETTY FAST. SAVE YOURSELF SOME MONEY AND JUST FORGET ABOUT A CAR IF...

**THE CAR LOOKS LIKE A WRECK.**
You can tell a lot just by standing back and squinting. Seriously. If the overall impression you get is bad, it's safe to assume this car is not a diamond in the rough.

**IT'S REALLY RUSTY.**
Rust eats at a car like termites eat wood. Once it gets going it's very hard to contain, so even relatively minor rusting means there might be more you can't see.

**THERE ARE HINTS IT'S BEEN TOTALED.**
Crooked doors, loose handles, major dents and big old scratches could indicate the car has had a near-death experience.

**SEVERE STAINS INSIDE POINT TO WATER DAMAGE.**
Cars can't swim.

**SOMEONE'S BEEN MONKEYING WITH THE ODOMETER.**
Numbers that don't line up and scratches around the screw holes are signs that the odometer has been rolled back.

# 5 USED-CAR TRAPS TO AVOID

## 1 AUCTION GUIDES

Auction guides, which claim to give you privileged and specific information about when and where to get good deals at car auctions, are nothing but a scam. The information they provide is vague and publicly available, so don't give these people your credit card number.

## 2 BUYING AS-IS

When a car is sold as-is, the seller is basically saying "don't come crying to me." There is no warranty, nothing you can do if your car randomly explodes, and no guarantee that it will even run. This really isn't a trap you can avoid because all private sales are as-is. Dealers are required by law to post a Buyer's Guide on the car, a form with giant check-off boxes that explain whether the sale is as-is or if the car is under some form of warranty.

*Talk about sticker shock!*

## 3 STOLEN CARS

The problem with stolen cars is, well, they're stolen. Here are some signs a car may be stolen: The VIN on the title doesn't match the one on the car; the VIN is gone; the license plate is brand new; the original keys are unavailable; the car is way too cheap; the car used to be your car before it mysteriously went missing last week. Check the VIN with your local DMV, or get a Carfax report, to be sure you're not making a hotter deal than you can handle.

## 4 SALVAGED CARS

If a car is wrecked so badly that the insurance company declares it a total loss, it's sold at auction and retitled with a salvage title. Salvaged vehicles can sometimes slip back onto the market in other states with clean titles, and although they might look good as new they often have major problems. Order a Carfax report to make sure the car you're buying isn't damaged goods.

## 5 LEMONS

Lemons, like salvaged cars, often make their way onto used car lots posing as regular old innocent used cars. If a car is less than a year old but already for sale again, it might be a lemon. A Carfax report will keep you from buying someone else's nightmare.

**FIND OUT MORE ABOUT CARFAX REPORTS AT REALUGUIDES.COM.**

**FUN**

SIGN HERE

GREAT
INTEREST
RATES!

# WITH FINANCING!

## Getting a good deal on auto financing is all about two things:

First, you have to understand how auto loans work, and then get down and dirty with some numbers. Fortunately, the math isn't as scary as you might think. Second, you need to shop around to find the best possible deal. First-time buyers are often at a disadvantage, but if you understand what you're up against, you can still buy a car and not end up living out of it.

### ANATOMY OF AN AUTO LOAN

A car loan consists of a number of variables including:

**The cost of the car.**
Be sure to include taxes and fees.

**The size of your down-payment.**
The more cash you put down up front, the less you have to finance, and the less interest you have to pay.

**Your APR.**
The lower your annual percentage rate, the lower your monthly payments, and the less you pay over the long haul.

**The length of the loan.**
Car loans are usually two to five years. The longer the term of the loan, the lower your monthly payments will be. But do you really want to pay for that thing till the next Olympics rolls around? And then some?

**The size of your monthly payments.**
The more you can pay per month, the quicker you pay off your loan, and the less you'll pay in interest.

# Rules of Thumb

We're not the boss of you, but here's what the experts recommend you do to stay within your means when buying a car.

### PUT 20% DOWN

If you can't come up with this much at the beginning, you run the risk of being "upside down" in your loan, which is a lot less fun than it sounds. It means that the amount you owe on your car is more than the car itself is worth. (See example below for the sad details.) Making a 20% down-payment helps you avoid this.

### FINANCE FOR FOUR YEARS

Five max. Three? Even better if you can swing it. Longer loans cost you more, and leave you vulnerable to driving upside down.

### LIMIT PAYMENTS TO NO MORE THAN 20% OF YOUR MONTHLY INCOME

When we say "no more than" we mean you might want to figure on spending even less. Make sure you leave a buffer zone for pocket money, unforeseen circumstances, and that sweet cellular plan you've been eyeing.

*Don't do it!*

### Driving Upside Down

The day you drive a $20,000 car off the lot, its value drops to about $17,000. Let's say you only put $1000 down on that baby. You still owe $19,000—right? But if the car is stolen or totaled in a wreck, your insurance company will only cough up what the car was worth—the $17,000. So you end up owing $2000 to the bank for a car that's kicked it.

# Check It Out: Sample Car Payments on a $15,000 Loan

**Let's say you want to buy an $18,750 car, and like a good girl, you've put 20% down. Your car loan is $15,000. Good start!**

Now all you need to do is set up some financing. Check out this chart which shows you what your monthly payments will be, and the total amount you'll end up paying, for a variety of different interest rates and loan terms. And don't ignore the column that shows you how much you're really paying overall for the fifteen thou.

| | 2 YEAR LOAN | | 3 YEAR LOAN | | 4 YEAR LOAN | | 5 YEAR LOAN | |
|---|---|---|---|---|---|---|---|---|
| Interest Rate | Monthly Payment | Total Paid | Monthly Payment | Total Paid | Monthly Payment | Total Paid | Monthly Payment | Total Paid |
| 4% | $651 | $15,632 | $443 | $15,942 | $339 | $16,256 | $276 | $16,574 |
| 5% | $658 | $15,793 | $449 | $16,184 | $345 | $16,581 | $283 | $16,984 |
| 6% | $665 | $15,955 | $456 | $16,427 | $352 | $16,909 | $290 | $17,399 |
| 7% | $672 | $16,118 | $463 | $16,673 | $359 | $17,241 | $297 | $17,821 |
| 8% | $678 | $16,281 | $470 | $16,921 | $366 | $17,577 | $304 | $18,248 |
| 9% | $685 | $16,440 | $477 | $17,171 | $373 | $17,917 | $311 | $18,682 |

# FINANCING

# the DONT'S...

### 0-0-0 DEALS

Judging from the hyped and excited announcers who advertise these deals on TV, it sounds like they're giving the cars away for free. But listen carefully: They are offering "0 down, 0% and 0 payments for one year." After that one blissful year is over, reality sets in. You now owe all the payments you've postponed, sometimes with the interest they claimed didn't exist. Then you have to start making regular payments, and the interest rate on those is way higher than 0%. And you already know you shouldn't buy a car with 0 down. Unless you're planning on winning the lottery in a year, stay away from this "deal."

### OBSESSING OVER MONTHLY PAYMENTS

Obviously, the amount of your monthly payments is important. But if you focus only on monthly payments and ignore things like APR and the length of the loan, you can wind up paying more than you realized for a car you can't honestly afford. If the payments were spread out over a long enough period of time, you could "afford" a car that flies—but you'd be paying for it till your kids put you in an old age home.

### LOW FINANCING LURES

Many inexperienced buyers see offers for low or 0% APRs and rush to the dealership in a hot sweat, clutching their piggybanks, only to learn they don't qualify for that loan—or the car they want isn't available with that deal. But hey—as long as they're there, they buy a car anyway, which is exactly what the dealership was counting on! These deals are usually only for certain models, with certain downpayments, and for "qualified buyers" which usually means people with perfect credit.

### FIRST-TIME BUYER FINANCING

Although it'd be nice if they'd cut you a break since you're just starting out, the kind of first-time buyer financing dealerships offer has a higher APR than plain old financing. If you have poor credit, it might be the best you can do, but you have to shop around to be sure. Exception: Some first-time buyer programs offered by manufacturers to recent college graduates really are a better deal. If you're fresh out of college, check to see if an offer like this applies to the car you want.

# DO'S&DONT'S

## CREDIT LIFE INSURANCE AND OTHER INSURANCE

This is insurance that covers your car payments if you lose your job, die, or become disabled. Although this coverage may be useful in some cases, you can get it much cheaper from your insurance agent. Don't believe a salesperson who says you have to buy credit insurance in order to be approved for a loan—it's actually illegal for lenders to make this a requirement.

## "SUBJECT TO FINANCING APPROVAL…"

Never ever drive away in a new car until your financing is set in stone and you've got your signed contract. Read the fine print and look for anything that says your financing is subject to approval. Slimy dealerships might quote you a low rate, let you take the car home, and then call a week later to announce that the financing fell through and your new rate is much higher. At this point you're pretty much out of luck—dealerships have lousy return policies.

## PRE-PAYMENT PENALTIES

You want to be able to pay off your loan early, which can save you a fortune in interest. Make sure your lender won't charge you extra for doing so.

## ADJUSTABLE-RATE LOANS

These wallet drainers get you started with a great low APR that can then rise to something much less friendly over the life of the loan. If you go this route, make sure there's a reasonable limit to how high the rate can climb.

We don't want to hurt your feelings, but you probably aren't most lenders' idea of a hot prospect. You're young, maybe a little green around the edges, and you probably don't have your dream job right now. Aww, don't look so sad, it could be worse. At least you don't have a mortgage payment and two kids in college…yet. Here's how to make the best of your youth.

## CHECK YOUR CREDIT REPORT

Lenders look at your credit score to decide whether to lend you money and how much to charge you. This number is based on the information in your credit report—stuff like how much money you owe, how many times your payments have been late, and so on. Your score has a big impact on the rates you qualify for. Really sleazy dealers sometimes lie to you about your score to make you pay higher rates, so you need to check your credit before you start shopping for financing. To find out how to order, go to realuguides.com.

## BORROW FROM YOUR GRANDMA

Family members, especially your own, tend to have the very best interest rates. See if Granny's feeling charitable toward her favorite grandchild.

## DRESS THE PART

If you visit banks in the flesh, attempt to project the image of a responsible and mature adult. Put on a tie and brush your hair. At the very least, tie those shoes.

## CONSIDER CO-SIGNING

If you're still in your teens, lenders will probably want a parent to commit to the loan with you. This will go on your mom's credit report and affect her credit score too, so make sure you ask her real nice.

*she loaned me the money.*

*My best pants!*

## HANG ON TO YOUR JOB

Lenders are looking for stability. They like it if you have a job, and if you've had the same one for a year or so, that's even better.

## REFINANCE LATER

If you can't get a rate that's as low as you'd hoped, don't despair. You may be able to refinance later if your credit score improves. Of course, you don't want to commit to a terrible rate, because there's no guarantee this will work.

# Shop Around For Financing

Not all financing is created equal. Different lenders charge different rates, so you have to shop around. Here's a who's who of the auto loan world.

### Banks & Finance Companies
These guys compete with each other for your business, and often have good rates. Your own bank may be nicer to you, so definitely start there.

### Online Lenders
Online finance companies are convenient and competitive. You can apply for a loan online and have a blank check mailed to you if you qualify. As with any online transaction, be sure to shop smart. Deal with well-known companies and do background checks if you aren't sure.

### Credit Unions
Credit unions usually offer the lowest rates around, but they only lend to members. If you belong to a credit union, go there first.

### Dealerships
The important thing to know about financing through a dealership is that they don't lend you the money themselves. Instead, they pass your loan on to a lender, taking a percentage of the interest for themselves. Since they make more money if your rates are higher, it's foolish to just assume they're offering you the best rate possible. The exception to this rule occurs when manufacturers offer low interest rates, or even 0% financing, to help sell certain models.

# ALL ABOUT INSURANCE

**Until now, you've been driving an old rusty deathtrap that embarrassed your prom date and alienated your high school friends— and that was six years ago. You probably haven't been carrying insurance to replace that junker in case it got wrecked or stolen. Why bother—right?**

But now that you've bought your first real car—or at least a car that's worth more than an expensive dinner—you're going to need a complete insurance package. And if you're under 25 years old, it probably won't be cheap.

As always, we're here to help. Turn the page to find out how to decode the insurance terms and how to get the lowest possible rates.

# INSURANCE TERMS DECODED

## Auto insurance consists of a number of different types of coverage.

By law, you are required to carry liability, so that if you smack into someone, your insurance will pay for their loss. If you're financing the car through a bank, the bank will require you to carry collision and comprehensive coverage, so that the insurance company will replace the car if it's wrecked or stolen. Here's the scoop on each type of coverage—and what you do or don't need.

*It was the pole's fault*

### Personal Liability

This covers your butt when you hurt someone else or someone else's car. Most states require it—you can look up your state minimums at www.ican2000.com/state.html. Higher liability coverage helps protect your personal assets, like your house, if you get sued. If you're saying "House? What house? You mean this cardboard box?" the minimum requirement is probably all you need.

### Medical Payments

Also known as personal injury protection, this insurance pays the doctor's bills if you get hurt in a crash. When deciding how much coverage to get here, check to see what the limits are on the medical insurance you (hopefully) already have.

### Uninsured & Under-insured Motorist Coverage

If you are hit by some jerk without insurance, or without enough insurance, this coverage helps out with medical payments, pain and suffering compensation, and sometimes with the cost of fixing your car. Given the number of deadbeats out there, this is probably a good idea.

### Collision and Comprehensive

If you hit something—be it a car, a tree, or the rocky gorge below the bridge you just drove off—collision goes toward repairing your car. Comprehensive pays out when something other than a crash—like a falling tree, a hailstorm, or an elephant loose from the zoo—damages your pride and joy. If your old clunker isn't worth much, collision and comprehensive may not be worth it. For a fairly new car, you'll want some collision coverage at the very least.

# How to Lower Your Premiums

**There are tons of things that affect the price of your insurance premiums. Some of them, like your age and your gender, you're pretty much stuck with. Other factors, however, are totally within your control. Here's how you can lower your rates.**

**1.** Choose a car the insurance companies like. In general, the more boring the car, the cheaper the insurance. You'll pay more to insure sports cars because they're usually driven more aggressively and stolen more often. Certain other cars warrant higher rates as well, including models that crash more often, suffer a lot of damage when they crash, or cause more injuries to their passengers and other cars when they're involved in a wreck. Ask your agent for rates on different models before you buy. Or head to edmunds.com, where the "cost of ownership" feature can give you a ballpark idea about insurance rates.

**2.** Choose safety features the insurance companies like. Most insurance companies offer discounts for safety devices such as ABS, automatic seatbelts, and front and side airbags. Security features also frequently qualify for discounts.

**3.** Drive safely. Insurance companies usually offer good driver discounts if you haven't been ticketed or been at fault in an accident.

**4.** Take a Driver's Ed course either at school or online. Some insurance companies will continue to give you a discount if you retake the course every 2 or 3 years. (Check with your insurance company first to make sure they recognize the online program you choose.)

**5.** If you're in school, get good grades. Many insurers give good student discounts to high school and college students with a B average or higher.

**6.** Choose a higher deductible. The deductible is the amount you pay before the insurance kicks in. The money you'll save on premiums in 2 or 3 years will make up for the fact that you'll have to shell out more money if you do crash.

**7.** If you have homeowner's insurance or a renter's policy, insure everything through one company. It can save you a bundle.

**8.** If you're still in school you can probably be insured through your parents' policy, which can save you a whole lot...especially if they forget to make you pay for it!

**9.** AAA membership might get you a discount in some cases.

# THE TRUTH

I couldn't afford to buy, so...

# ABOUT LEASING

If you're debating whether to buy or lease, the short answer is: Buy. The long answer? Buuuuyyyyyy! Sure, we know why people get excited about leasing. Who wouldn't get buzzed about driving an upscale sports car or an awesome leather-lined SUV for low monthly payments, and then trading it in for a brand spankin' new model every few years? The thing is, those lower monthly payments are just money down the drain because at the end of the lease, you own nothing.

When you buy a car, you pay for the whole darn thing, and when you're done paying for it, you own it. Then you can keep driving it for as long as you like, payment free.

When you lease a car, you're basically renting it for a really long time. You have to take really good care of it, because it isn't yours at all. If you return it with scrapes and dings and too many miles, you pay big-time fees and penalties.

Yes, your monthly payments are lower if you lease, but at the end of the lease you're right back where you started: carless.

If all you want is the lower monthly payment part, buy a cheaper car or save up more cash for a down-payment. But if you're still tempted by leasing, check out the rest of this chapter for the whole story.

# See Dick Lease.
# See Jane Buy.
# See Dick Pay.

## DICK AND JANE ARE GETTING THE SAME $20,000 CAR. DICK WANTS TO LEASE. JANE WANTS TO BUY. SIX YEARS PASS. LET'S WATCH AND LEARN.

■ Jane puts $4,000 down and finances for four years with payments of $383 per month. She keeps driving the car for two years after that. In total, she's paid $22,394.

■ Dick's monthly payments for his three-year lease are $327, for a total of $11,772. After his lease is up, he leases a new car for the same amount and payment, bringing his total cost to $23,544.

■ After six years of driving, Jane has paid $1,150 less than Dick, which isn't eye-popping, especially if she had to shell out for a big repair. The main difference is that while Jane owns a car worth $7,217, Dick is once again in need of a vehicle. Even assuming she loses the $1,150 to repairs, she's still seven grand ahead.

## THREE MORE YEARS PASS, AND THE DIFFERENCES REALLY BEGIN TO SHOW

- After his third identical lease, Dick has spent a total of $35,316.

- Jane has been driving the same old car, and has added $3,000 in repairs to the original price tag, for a total of $25,394.

- Over nine years Dick has spent $9,922 more than Jane, and is on the market for a car once again. Jane might be getting a little tired of her car, but it's still worth at least $4,000. Which means she's almost $14,000 richer than Dick.

# Leasing Hazards

The leasing process is a minefield of penalties topped off with a healthy dose of confusion. Whee! But if you're determined to lease, here are a few things to watch out for.

- **Excessive wear and tear charges**
  You know how carefully you drove your mom's car the first time you borrowed it? Okay, how carefully you should have driven it? That's how you drive a leased car all the time, because it ain't yours. The leasing company that owns the car wants it back in tip-top shape, so if you return it too banged up you'll pay a hefty penalty.

- **Excessive mileage charges**
  Typically you can drive leased cars 12,000-15,000 miles a year. If you drive more than that, you owe a good chunk of change at the end.

- **Early termination penalties**
  If you develop an allergy to the car and want out of your lease early, you'll owe all your remaining payments plus penalties. Ouch.

- **It's easier to get ripped off**
  One of the biggest dangers of leasing is simply that it's so confusing. With its strange language and bizarre mathematical equations, the leasing process causes many shoppers to stick their fingers in their ears and hum loudly instead of trying to understand what's going on. Car salespeople think that's just swell.

- **Oops, I leased a lemon**
  In a few states, lemon laws don't protect people who lease, which means you may end up trying to fix a perpetually broken car that isn't even yours. Check out your own state's laws before you decide to lease.

# MORE REAL U...
## CHECK OUT THESE OTHER REAL U GUIDES!

### YOUR FIRST APARTMENT

Everything you need to know about moving out of the house and into your first apartment, including how to deal with landlords, how to dump your roommate, and much more!

### IDENTITY THEFT

Find out how to protect yourself from the #1 crime in the U.S. Includes expert advice about surfing the Internet without leaving a trail for the criminals to follow.

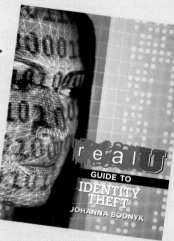

### PLANNING FOR COLLEGE

With a timeline for high school freshmen, sophomores, juniors, and seniors, this guide takes you step by step through the whole college selection and application process. Includes a clear and concise overview of financial aid, and much more.

## FOR MORE INFORMATION ON THESE AND OTHER REAL U GUIDES, VISIT WWW.REALUGUIDES.COM.